OCEANS

Library Edition Published 1990

Published by Marshall Cavendish Corporation
147 West Merrick Road
Freeport, Long Island
N.Y. 11520

Printed in Italy by Imago Publishing Ltd

© Marshall Cavendish Limited 1990
© Cherrytree Press Ltd 1989

Designed and produced by AS Publishing

Library of Congress Cataloging-in-Publication Data

Mariner, Tom
  Oceans / by Tom Mariner,
     p. cm. – (Earth in action)
     "A Cherrytree book."
  Includes index
  Summary: Explores the physical character of the world's oceans and how they interact with weather, the movements of the earth, and the life they support.
     ISBN 1-85435-190-7
     1. Oceans – Juvenile literature. [1. Oceans.]
I. Atkinson, Mike, ill. II. Title. III. Series: Earth in action
(New York, N.Y.)
GC21,5,M37 1989
551.46–dc20

89-9823
CIP
AC

· EARTH · IN · ACTION ·
OCEANS

Tom Mariner
Illustrated by Mike Atkinson

MARSHALL CAVENDISH
NEW YORK · LONDON · TORONTO · SYDNEY

Oceans of Life

Earth is a watery planet. Water in the oceans covers more than 70 percent of its surface. Water is present on earth in three forms. It is a solid when it freezes into ice; it is a liquid as water; and it is a gas when it becomes invisible water vapor in the air.

The water which fills the ocean basins makes it possible for life to exist on earth. The sun evaporates water from the oceans. The resulting water vapor rises to form the clouds, which are blown over the land. The clouds bring moisture to the land as rain or snow. Without moisture, there is no life.

The oceans are never still. They are agitated by waves, tides, and currents. Warm currents bring mild weather to some polar regions. Cold currents lower temperatures on coasts near them and chill onshore winds.

Studying the Oceans

In the last 40 years, astonishing discoveries have been made about the oceans. Much of the ocean floor has been mapped with instruments called echo-sounders. Scientists have been able to study samples of rocks from the ocean bed obtained by drilling. Research ships sail around the world, recording information about the oceans and the things that live in them.

People use the oceans in many ways. We eat the fish that live in them; we use them for transport and trade; for vacations and sports. We also use them as dumping grounds for our trash and sewage with too little care for their future and our own.

The deepest part of the ocean explored so far is in the Marianas Trench in the Pacific, which was visited by the bathyscaphe *Trieste*. Because of the extreme pressure of the sea, exploration has to be carried out in submarines or submersibles. Most research is carried out on the continental shelf, no deeper than about 1,600 feet (500 m). Divers supplied with oxygen and wearing armor-plated suits, may go as deep as 1,000 feet (300 m) but scuba divers can go down only about 100 feet (30 m) holding their breath.

submersible

1,500
(500)

5,000
(1500)

10,000
(3000)

15,000
(4500)

20,000
(6000)

25,000
(7500)

30,000
(9000)

35,000
(10,500)

Depth in feet
(meters)

Maps of the earth often give the impression that most of the earth's surface is dry land. In fact, more than two-thirds of the earth's surface is water. This view of the planet from over the Pacific shows how vast the ocean is.

The World of Water

The four main oceans are the Pacific, Atlantic, Indian, and Arctic. They are all joined and cover nearly 140 million square miles (360 mi sq km), 71 percent of the earth's surface. Recent estimates put the average depth of the oceans at 13,000 feet (3900 m), with a total volume of 321,400,000 cubic miles (1,285,600,000 cu km).

Some people talk of a fifth ocean, the Antarctic, or Southern, Ocean. But most geographers regard the waters around Antarctica as the southern parts of the Pacific, Atlantic, and Indian oceans.

Each ocean contains seas, bays and gulfs. Most of these areas of water are partly surrounded by land.

Seawater

Unlike the water in rivers and lakes, the water in the sea is salty and undrinkable. The average salinity (saltiness) is 3.5 percent. 2½ pounds (1 kg) of seawater contains 1¼ ounces (35 gms) of dissolved chemicals. 85 percent of them are sodium chloride (common salt).

Saline (salty) water is denser than fresh water. Cold water is denser than warm water. The temperature of seawater varies from 30°F ($-2°C$) (the freezing point of seawater) to almost 88°F (30°C) in warm, tropical seas.

The density of seawater is one of the reasons why water circulates continuously in currents. Cold, dense water sinks; warm, less-dense water flows on the surface. Water retains heat more easily than land, so warm ocean currents bring heat to lands which would otherwise be cold. Similarly, currents from polar regions bring cool onshore winds to tropical areas.

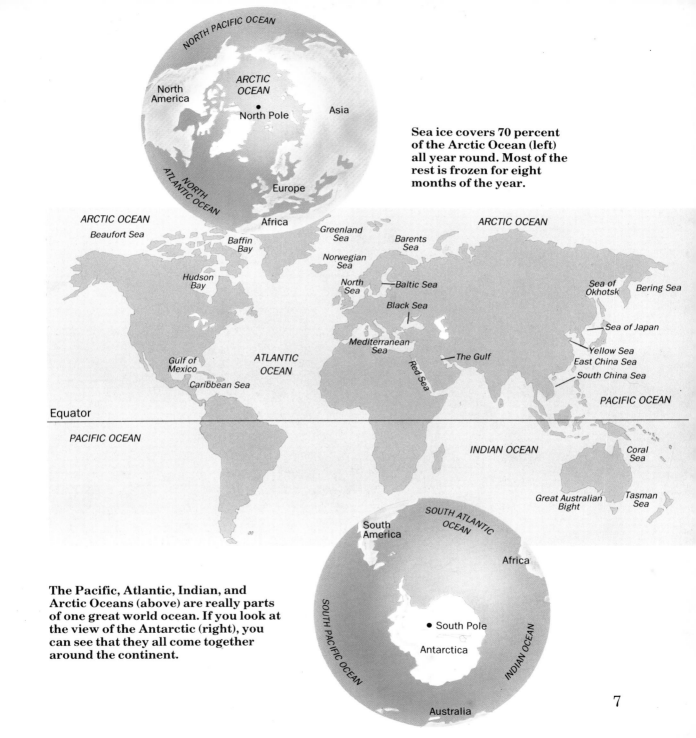

NORTH PACIFIC OCEAN

ARCTIC OCEAN

North America

Asia

North Pole

NORTH ATLANTIC OCEAN

Europe

Africa

Sea ice covers 70 percent of the Arctic Ocean (left) all year round. Most of the rest is frozen for eight months of the year.

ARCTIC OCEAN

Beaufort Sea

Baffin Bay

Hudson Bay

Greenland Sea

Norwegian Sea

North Sea

Baltic Sea

Black Sea

Barents Sea

ARCTIC OCEAN

Sea of Okhotsk

Bering Sea

Sea of Japan

ATLANTIC OCEAN

Mediterranean Sea

Red Sea

The Gulf

Yellow Sea

East China Sea

South China Sea

Gulf of Mexico

Caribbean Sea

PACIFIC OCEAN

Equator

PACIFIC OCEAN

INDIAN OCEAN

Coral Sea

Great Australian Bight

Tasman Sea

South America

SOUTH ATLANTIC OCEAN

Africa

The Pacific, Atlantic, Indian, and Arctic Oceans (above) are really parts of one great world ocean. If you look at the view of the Antarctic (right), you can see that they all come together around the continent.

SOUTH PACIFIC OCEAN

South Pole

Antarctica

INDIAN OCEAN

Australia

7

The Birth of the Oceans

When the earth was formed, about 4,600 million years ago, there were no oceans. The planet was boiling hot. Its surface was covered with swarms of volcanoes which, for millions of years, spouted gas and water vapor into the atmosphere. Gradually, the planet cooled, and the thick cloud of water vapor condensed into rain. Water poured from the skies in a mighty deluge that lasted for thousands of years. It filled hollows in the earth's crust and formed the first oceans.

Across the Ocean Floor

Imagine that you are looking at an ocean basin which

The oceans are divided into three zones: the continental shelves, the continental slopes, and the abyss. The abyss contains plains, mountain ranges, volcanoes, islands, and deep trenches.

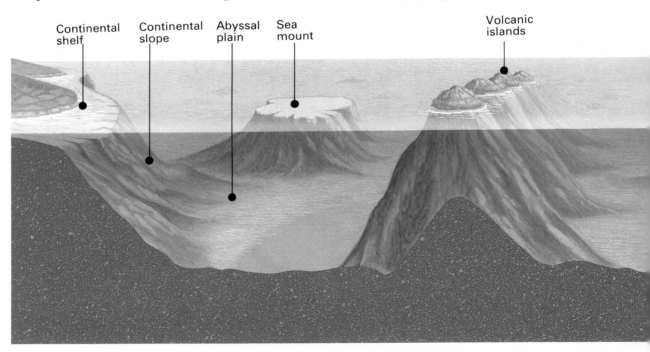

Continental shelf

Continental slope

Abyssal plain

Sea mount

Volcanic islands

has been drained dry. Around the continents is a gently sloping zone called the continental shelf. At the edge of this shelf is a steep continental slope, which falls sharply down to a flat plain. This is the abyss. The flat ocean floor is immense. It is broken by an occasional volcanic mountain or lines of islands topped by smoking volcanoes. Running as far as the eye can see, is a huge, broad mountain range, or ridge. This massive range is sliced by narrow canyons. Along its center is a long, deep valley.

Beyond the ridge lie more flat abyssal plains. Near the continent is a colossal trench, so deep and dark that the ocean bed seems to be plunging into the earth's interior.

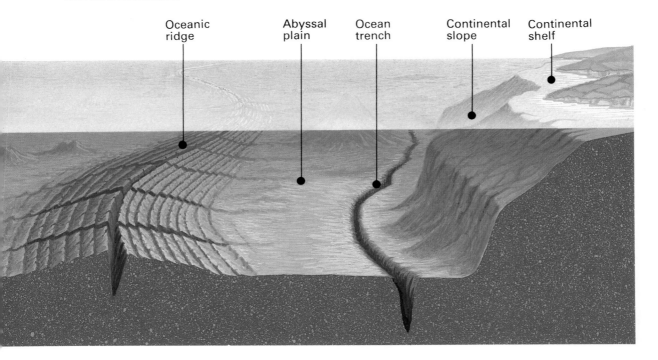

Oceanic ridge

Abyssal plain

Ocean trench

Continental slope

Continental shelf

The earth has three layers (above). The heavy *core* is made mostly of iron. Around it is a *mantle* of rock. Near the top of the mantle is molten rock called *magma.* A thin shell of rigid rock, consisting of the *crust* and the top layer of the mantle, floats on the magma.

The Spreading Oceans

The earth's crust is hard and thin. Beneath it is a zone of dense rock called the mantle, which surrounds the core. The crust is deeply cracked right down into the mantle. The cracks divide the outer layers of the earth into separate *plates*, which fit together like a jigsaw puzzle. The plates float on molten rock, called magma. Currents flowing in the hot magma make the plates move.

Making New Crust, Melting old Crust

When two plates drift apart, molten rock from a layer in the upper mantle oozes into the gaps. As it cools down, this magma hardens into new rock along the edges of the plates and becomes part of the crust. This is happening along the deep valley which runs through the center of the ocean ridges. The process pushes apart the plates on each side of the ridges, enlarging the oceans.

In other places, the crust is being melted, and then re-created, at roughly the same rate. Plates moved around by currents in the magma collide with others. When they do, one plate rides over the other. The lower plate is then thrust down into the mantle. As it descends, the edge of the plate melts. This is happening along the deep ocean trenches. Some of the melted rock rises up near the trenches to form volcanic islands.

One Continent, One Ocean

Now that scientists know how the plates move, they have been able to work out how the areas of ocean and land mass have gradually changed over millions of

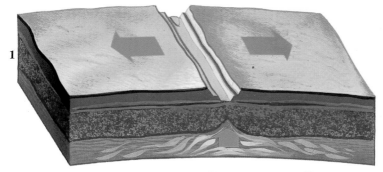

1

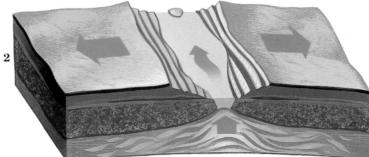

2

The birth of an ocean.
When plates under a
land mass move apart
(1), magma wells up from
below. It cools and
hardens to form new
crust. Water flows into
the depression (2) and
the new crust becomes
the bed of a new ocean.
This is happening in the
Red Sea, which is
widening by an inch or
so every year.

3

Through the center of
the long oceanic ridges
are deep cracks where
new rock is being formed
(3). Elsewhere, the edges
of plates are being
destroyed as they plunge
into deep trenches (4).

4

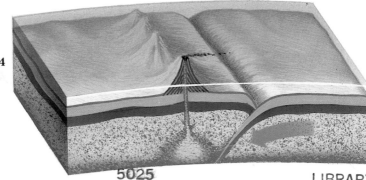

years. A split that continued to grow by about an inch a year would become an ocean 2,500 miles (4000 km) wide after 200 million years.

The strange fit between the coasts of Africa and South America was first noticed nearly 400 years ago. Modern computer maps of the edges of the continents (the continental shelves) show that they match exactly. Scientists calculate that about 200 million years ago, the continents were joined in a single supercontinent. This continent is called Pangaea, which means "all the earth". One vast ocean surrounded it.

About 180 millions of years ago, Pangaea began to break up, to form smaller new continents and smaller oceans. The continents are still drifting today, constantly changing the shape of the oceans.

On an ordinary map, the edges of the land masses look as if they might fit together. On a computer map of the continental shelves, which are the true edge of the continents, the fit is almost perfect. The continental shelves are shown in pale blue on this plan of how the continents fit together.

THE SLOWEST SHOW ON EARTH

In the early 1900s, earth scientists were puzzled by several questions. Why did the continents look as though they once fitted together? Why were fossils of identical plants and animals found in widely separated places? Why were fossils of tropical plants and animals found in the rocks of Antarctica?

A German scientist named Alfred Wegener tried to give the answers. He argued that once there had been a single huge continent. Millions of years ago, it split up and the pieces moved apart, carrying plants and animals with them. These pieces are the continents we know today.

This theory of continental drift answered the old questions, but raised a new one. How could the solid continents possibly move around the earth's surface? Wegener's own explanations were not convincing. People laughed at his theories, which were soon almost forgotten. Today, thanks to new studies of the earth's structure, we know that currents in the molten part of the mantle make the plates move, just as Wegener said they did.

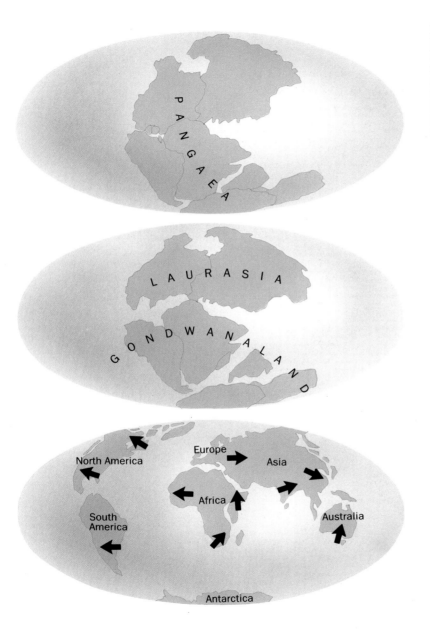

Earth scientists have been able to work out how the continents have moved during the last 200 million years. One vast continent, named Pangaea, was originally surrounded by one vast ocean (top).

This supercontinent began to break up about 180 million years ago (center). What are now North America, Europe, and most of Asia formed a land mass, named Laurasia, which drifted north. The rest made up Gondwanaland. Water from the one great ocean filled the hollow between the two continents.

About 130 million years ago, the outlines of the present continents had begun to take shape (bottom). The continents are still drifting today, so they and the oceans are continually changing shape.

Tides

Gravity is a force which all heavenly bodies exert upon each other. The moon's gravity exerts a pull on the earth and everything upon it. Solid things do not move much, but the seas and oceans do. Their waters are drawn into two bulges on opposite sides of the earth, one facing the moon, the other away from it. The moon drags the two bulges of water with it as it circles the earth each day.

Each time the earth revolves, it takes an extra 50 minutes to catch up with the moon, so high tides occur 50 minutes later each day. The sun affects the earth's tides less than the moon because it is farther away. But when moon and sun line up with the earth, which they do twice a month at full moon and new moon, their forces of gravity combine to produce very high

When the moon is in line with the sun, their forces of gravity pull together and cause high spring tides (left). When the sun, moon and earth form a right angle, lower neap tides occur (right). At the seashore, you can find out the time and height of the next tide from the tide gauge.

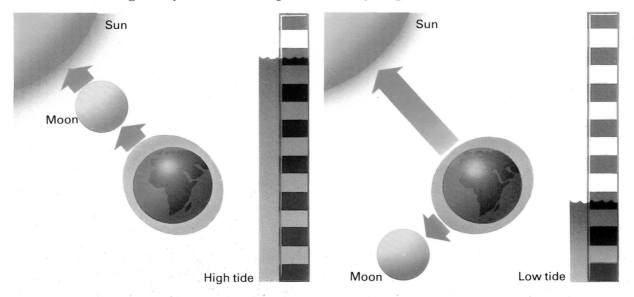

Sun

Moon

High tide

Sun

Moon

Low tide

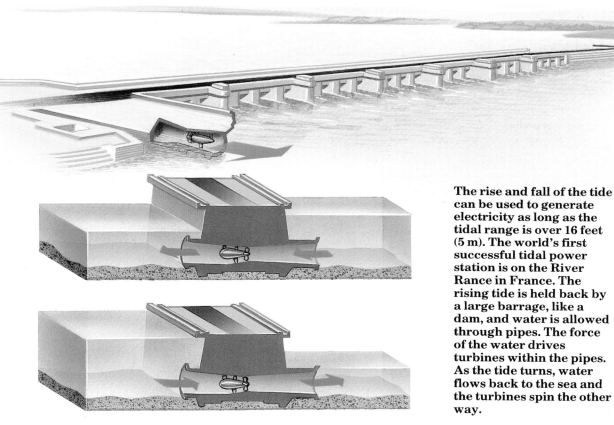

The rise and fall of the tide can be used to generate electricity as long as the tidal range is over 16 feet (5 m). The world's first successful tidal power station is on the River Rance in France. The rising tide is held back by a large barrage, like a dam, and water is allowed through pipes. The force of the water drives turbines within the pipes. As the tide turns, water flows back to the sea and the turbines spin the other way.

tides. These tides are called spring tides. The lowest tides occur when the sun and moon pull at right angles to each other, in the moon's first and third quarters. These tides are called neap tides.

Because oceans and seas differ in size, shape, and depth, tides also vary. In some places, there are tides, twice a day, in others only once, and in others there are no tides at all. The highest tides occur in the Bay of Fundy in Canada. Spring tides rise and fall by more than 50 feet (16 m).

15

Waves

Waves begin as ripples caused by wind blowing over water. The wind catches the ripples and whips them up into waves. The size and power of a wave depends on the speed of the wind, and the distance and length of time the wind has blown over the water. A wind blowing fast across a great mass of water, like an ocean, builds up the biggest waves.

Out at sea, waves do not move water forward. Instead, particles of water move round and round in circles as the wave passes through. This means that a cork in the sea bobs up and down, but stays in more or less the same position, unless it is moved by the wind or a current.

Waves are set in motion by the wind. Out at sea, each wave crest lifts water particles as it passes. The particles move forward, down, and back again in a circle. The movement triggers a similar movement below, so that there is a stack of smaller circles. When the waves reach shallow water, which is less than half the length of the wave deep, the circles flatten out.

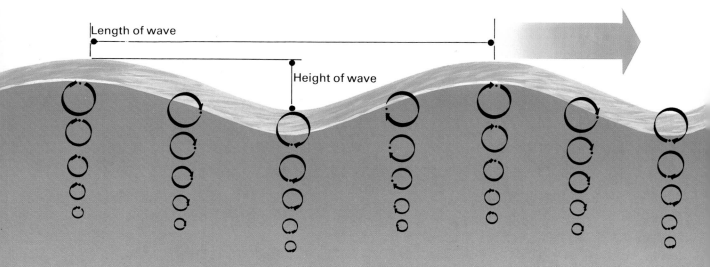

Length of wave

Height of wave

When the wave reaches a sloping beach, the water drags on the sea bed. The wave crests move closer together until the surface water topples forward, and breaks on the seashore.

If you see waves with steep sides and a choppy appearance, they are young waves that have been whipped up by local storms. If you are on a coast facing the open ocean, you may see waves which roll toward the land as a deep, heaving swell with intervals of ten seconds or more between their peaks. As they reach shallow water, they rear up, curve forward, and crash onto the shore. Waves like those have traveled a great distance. For example, waves that break on the coast of California in summer may have begun in winter storms near New Zealand, 6,000 miles (10,000 km) away.

TSUNAMIS
Tsunamis are waves caused by earthquake shocks or volcanic eruptions on the sea floor. These waves fan out in all directions, traveling at great speeds for enormous distances. In the deep ocean, a tsunami may make only a slight swell on the surface. But when it nears a shallow coast, it can rear up into a terrifying wall of water 200 feet (70 m) high.

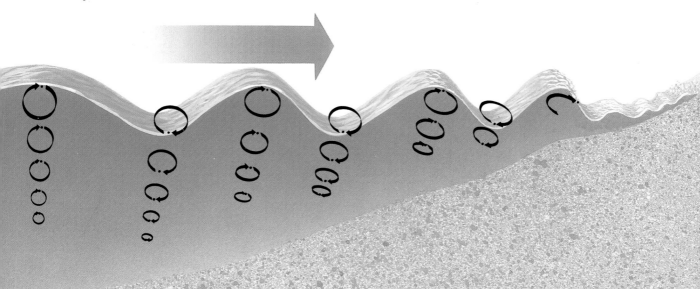

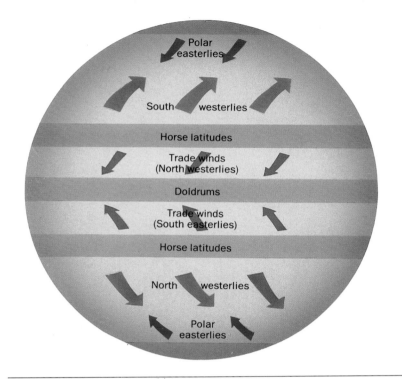

Polar
easterlies

South   westerlies

Horse latitudes

Trade winds
(North westerlies)

Doldrums

Trade winds
(South easterlies)

Horse latitudes

North   westerlies

Polar
easterlies

Ocean Currents

The sun warms the earth unevenly. About three times as much heat arrives at the equator as at the North and South Poles. Winds and currents absorb heat in equatorial regions and lose it, little by little, as they move toward cooler regions.

Steady, or prevailing, winds which blow most of the time, for most of the year, cause surface currents in the ocean. The spinning motion of the earth causes the currents to veer from their paths. North of the equator they curve to the right, south of it to the left. Other currents flow deep down in the oceans, often in the opposite direction to those on the surface.

Currents on the surface of the sea are caused by winds. Winds blow from areas of high pressure to areas of low pressure. Hot air at the equator rises and creates areas of low air pressure, called the doldrums. The rising air cools and spreads out to the north and south, where it sinks and becomes warmer, causing areas of low pressure, called the horse latitudes. The warm air flows toward the equator in winds called trade winds.

On the map (opposite), the red arrows show warm currents and the blue arrows cold currents. In the North Pacific and North Atlantic Oceans, the currents move in a clockwise direction. In the South Pacific and South Atlantic, they move in a counterclockwise direction.

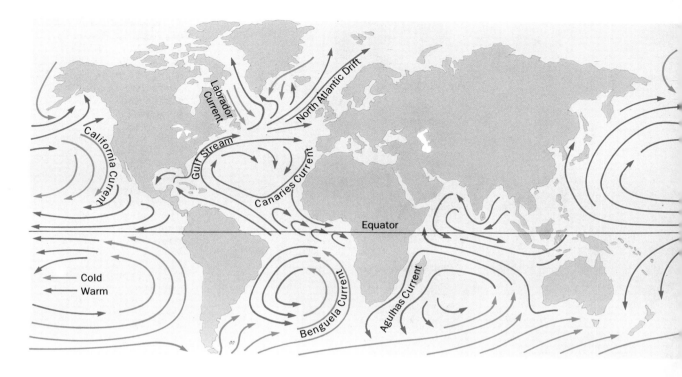

Cold
Warm

Warm currents flowing away from the equator are matched by cold currents bringing water from the poles to the equator. Cold water is heavier than warm water. Continual cooling at the poles causes water there to sink. This deep water moves slowly. It may take hundreds of years on its journey, but in places, some of it comes to the surface. This happens when offshore winds push the top layer of water away from the land. The deep, cold water wells up to replace it and continues to drift, as surface currents, toward the equator. The warm and cold currents form vast spirals of water on both sides of the equator in the three main oceans.

THE GULF STREAM
The Gulf Stream is an unusually rapid current. Trade winds push warm, tropical water into the Gulf of Mexico. This water spills out past Florida as a warm current 40 miles (60 km) wide. Westerly winds push it to northern Europe, where it becomes the North Atlantic Drift.

Oceans and Climate

The oceans regulate the climate of the earth. They receive energy in the form of heat from the sun. They store it, and circulate it around the earth. The oceans do not absorb the sun's heat evenly. Water in polar regions is cold, and vast areas of the surface are frozen over, while at the equator, the surface water is always warm. Yet the poles do not get colder and colder, and the water at the equator does not get progressively hotter. Both stay much the same. The balance is maintained by ocean currents. Warm currents starting near the equator flow away from it, transferring heat toward the poles. Cold currents flow from the poles to cool the warm waters near the equator.

Heat from the sun penetrates deep into water, but reaches only the top few inches of soil or rock. The oceans therefore absorb much more of the sun's energy than the land.

Land, Air, and Ocean
Winds blowing over the oceans are warmed or cooled by the water, and these winds raise or lower temperatures over the land. In the North Atlantic Ocean, winds coming off the cold Labrador currents chill the

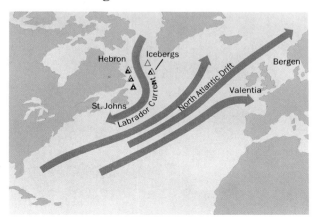

TEMPERATURE CONTRASTS
Ocean currents greatly affect the temperature of the land. Places in the same latitudes that you would expect to have the same temperature may vary enormously. Hebron −6°F (−21°C), Bergen 37½°F (3°C), St. Johns 23°F (−5°C), Valentia 45°F (7°C); these are average January temperatures from these towns. The cold Labrador current cools Hebron and St. Johns, while the North Atlantic Drift warms Bergen and Valentia.

eastern coasts of North America, while western Europe is warmed by air that has passed over the North Atlantic Drift. The North American coasts have long, cold winters, while winters in most of western Europe are mild.

The oceans, the atmosphere, and the land are linked by the water cycle. This cycle begins when air moving over the ocean picks up moisture in the form of water vapor. Winds carry the vapor to the land. The air rises and the water vapor turns into masses of water droplets, or clouds. The clouds release the moisture, which falls to the earth as rain or snow. The cycle ends, and then begins again, when the water flows back to the oceans through rivers.

The water cycle is powered by the sun. Water from the surface of the oceans evaporates. Laden with water vapor the hot air rises and is blown over the land by the wind. As the air rises, the vapor condenses and forms clouds. Rain or snow falls from them to the ground. The water eventually drains into rivers and flows back to the sea.

Life in the Sea

The blue whale is the largest creature that has ever lived. Its tongue alone weighs nearly as much as an elephant. Yet it feeds on plankton, which are some of the tiniest living things in the ocean.

There are three kinds of life in the sea: plankton, nekton, and benthos. Phytoplankton are the basic foodstuff of the ocean. They are microscopic plants which use energy from the sun to transform water and minerals into vegetable food. Multitudes of tiny animals called zooplankton browse on the phytoplankton. Plankton means "wanderer", and both kinds drift wherever the sea takes them.

Plankton

Hunters and Hunted

The nekton are free-swimming creatures. They include most fishes, dolphins, whales, seals, squid, and reptiles, such as sea snakes and turtles. The nekton are hunters and feed mostly on each other. Some, including the larger whales, live by gulping down huge quantities of plankton.

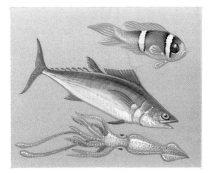
Nekton

The benthos are creatures of the sea floor. Lobsters and crabs move about to catch their food. Sponges, sea anemones, and sea-mats are anchored to the sea bed; they look more like plants than animals. The anemones open their "petals" to catch prey; the others live on decaying matter which drifts down from the sea above.

In the depths of the sea, where no light penetrates, strange carnivorous fishes live, including the deep sea angler. It has a long fin on its head which acts as a fishing rod. A luminous bait on the end attracts fish to the rod, and the angler snaps them up.

Benthos

Life in the sea is immensely varied. There are more than 14,000 kinds of fish, from huge sharks and sunfish to tiny anchovies. The largest animals are the whales. Despite their size, some of them live on the tiny planktonic plants and animals which swarm in the surface waters.

All marine life depends on light – and heat – from the sun, the pressure of the water, and the food supply. Most of the free-swimming creatures that make up the nekton feed on each other.

Bottom-dwelling benthos are often anchored to the sea bed. They eat live food or scraps of dead food that sink to the sea bed.

In the depths of the ocean where no light penetrates, the fish carry their own lights, so that they can see and be seen. They can tolerate great pressure; all of them are carnivorous.

The Food Cycle

Plankton is the basis of the ocean food web. Phytoplankton make their own food in the way that land plants do. They enrich the sea with oxygen and provide food for the swarms of plankton animals – the zooplankton. Fish, such as herring, feed on the zooplankton, and are in their turn eaten by cod, dolphins, sharks, and tuna.

Scraps of dead animals and plants in the upper waters sink to the sea bed in a continuous rain. Some are eaten by bottom-dwelling creatures. The rest is broken down by bacteria into nutritious compost. Cold

Millions of microscopic plants float in the sea. They are grazed on by a host of microscopic animals – mostly tiny shrimp called krill. Together, they make up the plankton. Herring feeds on the plankton and are themselves eaten by cod. The starfish eats the leftovers. This simple sequence is a food chain. Herring and cod are also eaten by numerous other animals, including sharks and humans. Simple food chains woven together form food webs.

currents churn up these deposits and bring them to the surface. Wherever this food appears, phytoplankton grows so fast that the sea is colored by it. This is followed by a huge increase in the zooplankton, which in turn becomes food for vast shoals of fish.

Those areas where food for plankton is swept to the surface are the main fishing grounds of the world. Plankton is far more plentiful in cold waters than in warm, which is why Arctic and Antarctic waters are the best fishing grounds for people — and for the great whales that live on the fish or the tiny plankton.

Nets and lines are designed to catch particular kinds of fish. The trawl net is dragged along the sea bed to catch cod and haddock, and the bottom-dwelling flounder. Drift nets are like curtains to draw around surface shoals and trap them. Herring and sardine are caught this way.

Wealth from the Sea

The sea contains vast wealth which we are only now beginning to use. In a few places the power of tides is harnessed to provide electricity. Devices for harnessing wave power are being tested all the time to find ones that will provide an endless and economical source of power from the bobbing movements of the water. Another idea for using the power of the oceans is the thermal power station, which uses the difference between the warm surface water and the deep, cold water to generate electricity. No one has yet discovered how to make such a device work in practice.

Minerals

There are rich mineral deposits beneath the sea, and vast quantities of chemicals and minerals dissolved in it. More than a third of the world's oil comes from under the sea, but other minerals are mostly more difficult or more expensive to extract.

Sulfur, manganese, and other dissolved substances are washed into the oceans by rivers or thrown up by underwater volcanoes. A mineral like gold is present in such small concentrations – four grams in every million tons of seawater – that there is no point in trying to extract it. In contrast, most of the world's supplies of magnesium come from the sea. Magnesium is relatively plentiful, the process for extracting it is simple, and new methods are making the process even cheaper.

Bromine, which is used to make photographic film and anti-knock compounds in gasoline, is another valuable element extracted from the oceans.

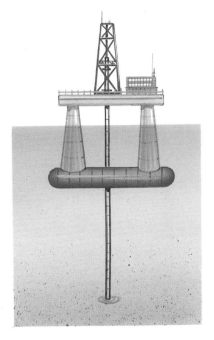

About a third of the world's oil comes from wells drilled in the floors of shallow seas around the continents.

Dredgers (right) scoop up sand and gravel in shallow water just offshore. Minerals are also dredged in this way, though special dredgers are needed for work in deep water.

In the 1970s, vast sheets of smooth, black, potato-sized pebbles were detected on part of the deep sea bed. They turned out to be lumps, or nodules, of manganese which also contain nickel, cobalt, and copper. These metals are so valuable that special dredgers have been designed to scoop up the nodules, which lie more than 10,000 feet (3000 m) down.

Salt and Water

To maintain life on land, plants and animals need fresh water. In areas where little fresh water exists, great efforts are made to desalinate (remove the salt) from sea water. Common salt (sodium chloride) is the most abundant substance in sea water. Even so, less than a third of the world's salt comes from the sea. Most is mined on land from deposits laid down by ancient seas millions of years ago. It is cheaper to get it that way.

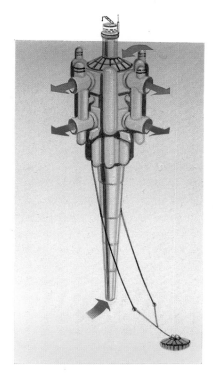

In this giant float 1,650 feet (500m) deep, warm surface water vaporizes ammonia. The gas operates turbines, which generate electricity. Deep cold water condenses the gas and repeats the process. The device is part of the Ocean Thermal Energy Conservation project.

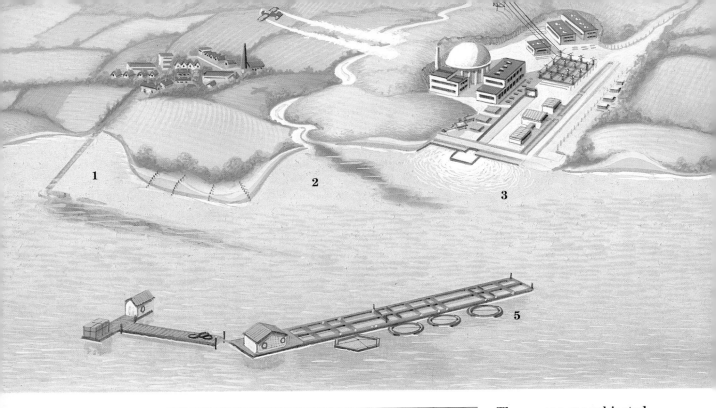

Seas or Sewers?

Because the oceans are so vast, people have always used them as dumping places, casually spilling sewage, lethal chemicals, nuclear waste, oil, and garbage into the water. In doing so, they destroy the delicately balanced patterns of marine life. They kill millions of sea creatures and poison the people who eat them. All around the world, beaches are polluted and coastal waters are unfit to swim in.

More than 3½ million tons of oil are deliberately spilled in the oceans annually. In addition, there is accidental spillage from wrecked tankers or oil platforms. Poisons in the oil sink into the oceans and

The oceans are subjected to much abuse. In some places, raw sewage and waste from towns (1) is piped out to sea. Fertilizers and pesticides, full of harmful chemicals used on the land (2), drain into rivers. Nuclear power stations (3) may pump contaminated water into the sea, and dump radioactive waste in metal containers. How long the containers will last, nobody knows.

Industries of all kinds (4) dump dangerous waste into the water. Fish farms (5) pollute the water with their waste. Oil spilled from rigs and tankers (6), often deliberately, is a hazard to all marine life. Oil kills a million birds every year. Fishing has become such an efficient industry, and people are so greedy, that many fish are becoming scarce (7).

destroy undersea life, while sea birds are killed at a rate of more than a million a year.

Fortunately, people are now aware that polluted seas are lethal and are taking action to make the seas clean and safe. A majority of nations with nuclear industries have agreed to stop dumping nuclear waste in the ocean deeps. The 17 Mediterranean countries have combined in a unified program to clean up their dangerously polluted sea. Other areas in danger have made similar plans. New ships have been designed to prevent accidental oil spillage. Many governments are also cooperating in action to prevent over-fishing, which threatens many species of fish and whales with extinction.

Ocean Futures

The world's population is increasing quickly. More resources and food, and more energy and living space, are needed. The ocean's resources should be able to satisfy the extra needs. Scientists do not yet know how to use the resources at reasonable cost. But they are learning every day from the new underwater technology created for the oil industry, from successful experiments to farm fish and seaweed, and from continuing undersea research.

Some people dream of building cities under the sea, but the problems of breathing and adapting to pressure are immense. Seabed laboratories and workshops, where scientists and technicians stay for short periods, are a reality, but few believe that people will ever be able to live under the sea.

Seabed research stations like this, where people live and work at depths of about 150 feet (50 m), help us to learn more and more about the oceans.

Ocean Profiles

Arctic Ocean
The Arctic is a small, cold, shallow ocean around the North Pole. It is bordered by the northern coasts of North America, Asia and Europe. The narrow Bering Strait links it with the Pacific. Several wider channels and the Norwegian Sea link it to the Atlantic. In winter, the ocean is frozen, but in summer, some of the ice breaks up.

Atlantic Ocean
The Atlantic connects the two polar regions, and is bordered by North and South America in the west and Europe and Africa in the east. It is fringed by several shallow seas, including the Caribbean, Mediterranean, and Baltic Seas. The area north of the equator is known as the North Atlantic, the area south of it, including the Antarctic area, is known as the South Atlantic. Second largest of the oceans, the Atlantic's area is 31,650,000 square miles (82,000,000 sq km), its average depth 11,000 feet (3310 m). Running north-south through its length is a huge oceanic ridge, which rises as islands in several places.

Indian Ocean
The Indian Ocean is bordered by the coasts of eastern Africa, southern Asia, and western Australia. It lies almost entirely south of the equator and is linked to the Pacific and Atlantic oceans around Antarctica. It is linked to the Mediterranean Sea via the Red Sea and the Suez Canal. Third largest of the oceans, its area is 30,000,000 square miles (76,000,000 sq km).

Pacific Ocean
The Pacific lies between North and South America in the east and Asia and Australia in the west and stretches from the Arctic to the Antarctic, where it is linked to the Atlantic and Indian Oceans. North of the equator, it is the North Pacific, south of it, the South Pacific. Its area is 64,000,000 square miles (166,000,000 sq km). It contains the deepest point so far measured, about 36,000 feet (11,000 m) in the Marianas Trench, and the highest underwater mountain, nearly 30,000 feet (8700 m) near the Tonga Trench. It contains thousands of islands, many of them volcanic.

Index